21st-century's Most Inspirational Songs

21st-century's Most Inspirational Songs

Table Of Contents

Foreword

It does not matter what sort of music inspires you, it's what it does to you that counts. Music may open your eyes, cause you to think, make you think more profoundly. Music may energize you, fill otherwise void moments, and keep you company.

Perhaps your life has you tied up in tangles. Music may help you come through your day, loosen up, solve your troubles, and just take that load off your brain. It may inspire you to face yet some other day...

Music may mend. The right music may fill you with reverence and wonder, lift you out of your daily life and send you gliding with the angels. It may give you hope, perk up your imagination, and help you alter your life and then alter the world.

Most Inspiring Music Songs Of The 21st Century

Music That Will Fill Your Soul

Chapter 1:

Leave A Legacy – Aaron and Jeoffrey

Synopsis

Inspiration DNA's Main Theme Song.

Legacy

Father Jeoffrey Benward was already working in the Christian music scene since 1970. In the early on nineties, after asking his then adolescent son Aaron what he would like to do for a living, was amazed to determine that he wished to follow the same path in music.

They made a decision to start recording together, and although a lot of labels had troubles with the bizarre pairing, Starsong picked them up. They moved into the studio and began working on their eponymous launching album which was brought out in 1995. The album had guest vocals by dc Talk.

The pair followed with After the Rain in '96 and with Climb in '97. Not long after, both father and son chose to travel along their individual careers.

During their music calling, Aaron and Jeoffrey had fourteen Top Five radio singles, nine of which arrived at #1. Their record albums have sold more than a hundred thousand units. They were twice nominated for a Dove Award in the "Song of the Year" class for their classic "He Is."

As of late the song Leave A Legacy has been released and is now Inspiration DNA's main theme song. The song speaks to the power behind leaving a legacy. This song is inspiring as it causes you to think about the legacy you will be leaving behind in this world. What do you want the people around you to learn from you? Do you want to teach people to be responsible and diligent workers at whatever they do? Do you want to teach individuals to know that love and laugher are truly important? Do you want to teach people to understand that relationships matter most? Do you want to teach people that grace and love are 2 components to mix into the lives of other people and in their own lives?

Aaron says that one goal that is important is to show a positive parent/youngster relationship, and hopefully be a role model for fathers and their sons or parents and their youngsters.

The pair has taken to heart the final prophetic word of the Old Testament where it states in Malachi 4:6 that 'The fathers' hearts would be turned to their children and the children's hearts to their fathers, lest I smite them with a curse.' Every social issue that we face nowadays may be traced back to a dysfunctional family life. We need to address these problems.

This inspirational song does just that and can be heard here:

http://www.youtube.com/watch?v=eCMNjaIXjwA

Chapter 2:

Heal The World - Michael Jackson

Synopsis

"Heal the World" is a song from Michael Jackson's hit album, Dangerous, released in '91.

Help Others

The music video features children living in countries suffering from unrest especially Burundi. It is also one of only a handful of Michael Jackson's videos not to show Jackson himself.

In a 2001 Internet chat with admirers, Jackson said "Heal the World" is the song he is most proud to have created. He also created the Heal the World Foundation, a charitable organization which was designed to improve the lives of children. The organization was also meant to teach children how to help others.

The song is inspirational as it speaks to keeping a place in your heart for love for other people and helping to heal other people as well. The song was brought to fruition through Heal the World Foundation.

It was a charitable organization established by entertainer Michael Jackson in '92. The foundation's origination was prompted by the song of the same name. The aim of the charity was to supply medication to youngsters and battle world starvation, people being homeless, child victimization and abuse. Jackson said that he wished "to improve the conditions for children throughout the world".

The foundation in addition to all the things above brought underprivileged youngsters to Jackson's Neverland Ranch, which was located outside Santa Ynez, CA, to take a turn on theme park rides that the entertainer had constructed on the property after he bought it in '88.

With this foundation, Michael Jackson airlifted forty-six tons of provisions to Sarajevo, established drug and alcohol abuse training and donated 1000000s of dollars to deprived youngsters, including the entire payment of a Hungarian youngster's liver transplant.

As the adage goes, "charity begins at home." Make certain that your immediate loved ones have the first claim on your time and resources. After that, assist any acquaintances in need and you'll help the world close by.

A lot of youngsters both at home and abroad are in need of more beneficial care, including medical and dental care, apparel, training, and better nutrition. If assisting youngsters is a priority for you there are a lot of opportunities to get involved by donating time or revenue. If you assist youngsters, you assist the world and its future.

A lot of individuals are poor through no blame of their own and require help. Whether they're individuals in your own community or in a growing country, the chance to assist the world by giving to the poor forever seems to be available. Natural disasters and states of war alone deprive many thousands of families yearly.

Whether they're your own relatives or acquaintances, or are those who are alone in the cosmos, the sick need consoling and encouragement. A beneficial way to assist the world is to commit some of your time to visiting the ill.

Few matters are more deplorable than abused youngsters. Mistreated women are a close 2nd in their need for understanding and assistance. If you're in a position to assist abused youngsters or women then you'll help the world by correcting abominable wrongs.

One may hardly savor life, liberty and the pursuit of happiness when illiterate. You are able to assist those who can't read or write but would like to learn, either by donating time or by supporting worthwhile plans in your community. This is a capital way to assist the world.

Many of us have discovered over the years the worldwide need to engage in behaviors that assist our common surroundings. Fresh air, clean water, and decreases in waste benefit everybody. You are able to help by going green both at home and work. You'll be likely to save income, also.

The video that will completely touch your heart and fill your soul can be found here:

http://www.youtube.com/watch?v=BWf-eARnf6U

Chapter 3:

Can't Take That Away - Mariah Carey

Synopsis

*"Can't Take That Away (Mariah's Theme)" is a song authored
by American singer Mariah Carey and Diane Warren.*

Be Brave

The song is inspirational as it speaks to the battles of dealing with individuals who put you down, and how to defeat these battles through faith, courage, and the power of God. Carey explains in the song's lyrics how while individuals can attempt to make her feel down and blue, regardless what happens, she can not let them win: "There's a light in me that shines brightly. They can try but they can't take that away from me."

2 music videos were made for "Can't Take That Away," both orchestrated by Sanaa Hamri. The production of the video called for some of Carey's fans to take part. She called for them to participate via her site and asked them to send in video clips of themselves, stating the adversities in their lives and how "Can't Take That Away" had urged them on and inspired.

A competition was held, and video clips from 5 fans were selected for inclusion in the video recording. The clips were featured in the video's intro, where Carey responds to her fan's struggles which included personal insecurities, the troubles of being part of a racial or social minority, and being goldbricked by verbal harassment.

Have faith in yourself to succeed. Take a chance and know that you have your smarts, instinct and natural endowment on your side. Plus, your acquaintances and loved ones are there for you. Use your courage. It may be compared to a muscle. The more we utilize it, the stronger bravery gets.

Accept accountability for failure. This takes bravery and shows that you're a real leader. Understand that quitting isn't an option. It takes bravery to endure. It's much easier to quit. Being relentless despite disheartenment takes great courage. Battle to overcome your fear. Brave individuals might still be afraid, but the difference is that they subdue their fear. They do not let it hold them back. Rather, they use it as a reminder of what they may lose if they don't endure.

Follow up on your ideas. It takes bravery to put your trust in yourself. The worst conclusion you can make is to do nothing. Take chances and know that you are able to succeed.

Get courage by studying inspiring stories of brave individuals.

You can hear the inspirational message of this song here:

http://www.youtube.com/watch?v=XrebNpxGCMA

Chapter 4:

Imagine - John Lennon

Synopsis

"Imagine" is a song authored and performed by English rock and roll musician John Lennon.

Think Of It

The song's chorus might have been partly prompted by Yoko Ono's poetry in reaction to her childhood in Japan during the Second World War and is inspirational because it speaks of a world of peace.

Lennon said in an interview: It's not a fresh message: "Give Peace a Chance" — we're not acting absurd. Just stating "give it a chance." With "Imagine" we're inquiring, "can you imagine a world without countries or religions?" It is the same message again and again. And it is positive Ono suggested that the lyrical material of "Imagine" was "just what John trusted — that we're all one country, one creation, and one people. He wishes to get that idea out." In addition, the material of "Imagine" was the brainchild for the concept of Nutopia: The (fictional) Country of Peace, produced in '73.

We are all discussing it, but who's doing it? Begin now - world peace is conceivable, but it can't occur if any of us remain in opposition. Let go of little arguments, live your life, discover happiness. It's out there - trust me.

Smile At everybody. All of the time. You don't understand who they've lost, what they're enduring or how much their heart is breaking. Smile even if they are raging, sad or apathetic.

Ask little, forgive a great deal. Be generous with your affection; forgive individuals for being people, or for not being the individuals you wish them to be. Forgive them for the ways they're unlike you: dissimilar beliefs, dissimilar cultures, dissimilar loves, and another color.

Relinquish stuff 'cause you can't take any of it with you anyhow. So savor right now and forget about amassing wealth, possessions or anything else. You never know when your time is up anyhow, so savor your life with more heart and less stuff.

Treat every living thing with honor. Every creature just would like to be happy the same way you wish to be happy. Respect that. If you wouldn't wish it done to you, don't do it to anybody else. Discover love in every way you are able to and embrace it. More pleasure comes out of love than anything else. Stick up for those who can't stick up for themselves. The less attackable and more advantaged should protect the less forceful, not rule them. It's a weak ego that requires power over other people.

Do not defend violence, for any reason. There's nothing that warrants harming another individual. Particularly not money.

Yesterday is departed; tomorrow is an aspiration, live right now and pass the word. We can make a difference.

You can listen to this inspirational song here:

http://www.youtube.com/watch?v=okd3hLlvvLw

Chapter 5:

I Believe I Can Fly - R Kelly

Synopsis

"I Believe I Can Fly" is a song by R&B singer R. Kelly that came out in '96.

Soar

"I Believe I Can Fly" was number two on the Billboard Hot 100, number one on the R&B Singles chart, and number one on the United Kingdom charts. It's acquired 3 Grammys, and is ranked on Rolling Stone's list of the 500 Greatest Songs of All Time.

This song brings inspiration as it speaks of rising in the face of adversity:

> "If I can see it, then I can do it
> If I just believe it, there's nothing to it"

We're all confronted with adversity from the minute we're born into this world. Perhaps it's a physical, or psychological or financial hardship. What ever your burden might be, you'll be able to always rise above hardship by comprehending some common fundamental rules concerning how hardship plays a critical role in your life.

Individuals hear the word adversity and automatically believe that it's a foul thing, when in point of fact hardship is what furthers change and change is what induces growth. What ever your hardship is, realize it befriend it and do anything in your might to improve on that place in your life. Frequently our biggest adversaries in life become our most beneficial teacher.

Don't concern yourself with what you've no command over and substitute it for a need to enhance the matters you do have command over. Some of the greatest individuals in history came from really humble beginnings where they had to defeat huge hardships in their lives. How did they accomplish it? "The fact is that they recognized that in life, there are some things that just are and you are able to only proceed around them. The mystery is to not let them entirely obstruct your path to your goal.

Substitute hatred for understanding and impatience for tolerance. Initially it may seem really hard, But when you spend the time to know your adversary or enemy you recognize that they're you, just on the other side of the spectrum and you learn so much more about yourself in that practice.

Remember that you're not the first and you for sure won't be the last. Bask in the fact that, what ever it is that's holding you back is precisely what should be there, right now. Hardship isn't random, it's found to the rich, the misfortunate, the meager and the powerful throughout time. The only thing that differentiates these individuals is how they addressed with their own adversities.

You can hear this inspirational song here:

http://www.youtube.com/watch?v=16FdJrrAWSo

Chapter 6:

Jesus, Take The Wheel - Carrie Underwood

Synopsis

"Jesus, Take the Wheel" is a song authored by Brett James, Hillary Lindsey and Gordie Sampson. It's the first single from Carrie Underwood's introduction album, Some Hearts.

Let Go

The song recounts the story of a mom who lives a feverish life. On a late-night Christmas Eve drive on a snowy road on her way to Cincinnati, Ohio, the woman starts separating her emotions and deplores not having enough time to do the things that truly matter. Then, her auto hits a patch of black ice, inducing the woman to lose control of her auto. She panics, takes her hands off the wheel and cries out to Jesus; soon thereafter, the car quits spinning and safely comes to rest on the shoulder. After scrutinizing the state of affairs (and seeing that her child has remained sound asleep in the back seat), the woman resolves to let "Jesus take the Wheel" of her life.

This song is inspirational as it speaks to relinquishing matters to a higher power... whatever you choose to call that.

It comes to me that although I've never had a need or want to control others, for assorted reasons the need to be in control of me at all times has been nearly belligerent. In a lot of ways it's been a beneficial thing.

Regrettably, psychologically speaking there's a very human disposition to take a coping mechanism that works well in a few spots, and apply it to every situation. My disposition is to feel that if I'm not in total control and taking action, I'm not achieving anything. On a cerebral level I know this is untrue, since a lot of the best things in my life appeared to come to me in ways that were apparently unrelated (or even despite) any attempt on my part. Apparently there are times when it's good to "get myself out of the way" and let things take their course without attempting to micro-manage. Even so, for me this mindset of iron fisted self-command has reached areas where it's not so productive.

So it would appear now that I've discovered how to be in command, the following step is to discover how to purposely relinquish the need for control when it's good to do so.

One method is:

I wish you to consider the color of a ripe orange. Pretend a pool of orange light is washing your entire upper body, head, neck and chest. I want you to inhale orange light that holds surrender (relinquishing) and breathe out black which bears control. Do it once again, in orange and out black. Another time… Inward orange and away black. Now look the mirror and state "I relinquish to higher power and hold faith that everything will work out for the best. Relinquish, relinquish relinquish." State that mantra 3 times in the mirror. Do this each day and see if you can't relinquish control a bit better and discover some inner peace.

Some of you may choose the path of prayer… Choose what is most comfortable for you.

You can hear this inspirational message here:

http://www.youtube.com/watch?v=GkWw_xzxwJc

Chapter 7:

Wind Beneath My Wings- Bette Midler

Synopsis

"Wind Beneath My Wings" was performed by Bette Midler for the soundtrack of the movie Beaches and became a United States. Number 1 single. It was named Record of the Year and Song of the Year at the Grammy Awards of '90.

Show You Care

This song is inspirational as it speaks to showing appreciation and love for those around us.

"Did you ever know that you're my hero,
and everything I would like to be?
I can fly higher than an eagle,
'cause you are the wind beneath my wings."

Regardless how much individuals appreciate those significant to them, they frequently don't show their appreciation. Even if at heart individuals recognize they're appreciated, a sign of appreciation is always a kind gesture. It frequently doesn't take much to show somebody they're appreciated, it just takes choosing to do it and choosing how to do it.

Tell the individual how much you treasure him. You don't have to purchase expensive gifts or do anything out of the ordinary to show somebody your appreciation. Words can be adequate. Always thank individuals for the things they do and tell them you value them even when they have not exercised anything in particular.

Schedule a particular time with them. Spending time with somebody may be one of the most beneficial gifts you are able to give them. Take a day off work to spend with them or propose to take them out to lunch. Take them to certain place they like to go to, or take part in a special activity they like.

Provide a gift without an occasion. Rather than only giving gifts at the times of the year you're obliged to, give him a gift merely to show your appreciation. It doesn't have to be expensive as he'll feel good recognizing you thought of him. Attempt to find a little something he wouldn't purchase for himself, or make something as an alternative.

Do something without asking. Show your appreciation by attending to the youngsters for a day, fixing dinner for them or doing a certain chore she might dislike doing. This will let her understand you value all she does for you.

Make time to always hear. Showing appreciation doesn't have to be a one-time issue. You are able to show somebody you appreciate them daily by always making time for them whenever you are able to.

Centre on the great things. Nobody is perfect, but try to center on the favorable things individuals do. This will help you show appreciation.

You can see this inspirational message here:

http://www.youtube.com/watch?v=oiS8YokFzeY

Take time for someone today!

Chapter 8:

We Are the Champions - Queen

Synopsis

"We Are the Champions" is a power ballad authored by Freddie Mercury, recorded and performed by Queen for their 1977 record album News of the World. Among their most celebrated and popular songs, it's since become an anthem for sporting triumphs and has been frequently used or referenced in pop culture.

Keep Going

This song brings inspiration as it speaks of perseverance:

"We are the champions - my friends
And we'll keep on fighting - till the end -
We are the champions -
We are the champions
No time for losers
'Cause we are the champions - of the world"

Perseverance is a big word, and one that may be quite ambitious in the daily routines of life. Discovering to manage when it appears there's no way may be disheartening and seemingly out of the question. All the same, all things are possible to those whom dare to trust - it calls for perseverance!

The heavier the trial you're facing, the higher the reward will be for it. This is the time when you must dig your heels into the ground and stay firm - unmovable. If you feel yourself falling down or starting to slip, it's all right, as we all do. Pick yourself up and stand to persist.

Settle in your mind and arrive at the firm choice to do what you need to do and are going to accomplish whatever it is you're deciding in yourself to do. Enlighten yourself by becoming your own mentor and inspiration. There are going to be a lot of times when only you will understand what you're supposed to do and are trying to accomplish. So, you must discover to exclude and silence the many damaging voices you'll hear that state, "You recognize you can't do that, it's unimaginable ... You don't have .... You'll never ..." Rather, utilize the damaging voices and comments to make you even more driven to do what you're told will never occur - you are able to do it!

Don't overburden yourself, though, or you'll find yourself becoming easily disheartened from the weight of the overburden. You're only able to do particular amounts of things at one time, and you must take the steps essential to prevent this from happening but to let you do what you are able to in order to bring the goals to fruition.

Fire up the skills, powers and talents you bear deep inside you. This is a great time to take a very good look at yourself, literally. There are fresh ones ready to show up and be made known. What are the things you're good at executing? Listen to what other people say about you, and you'll start to see some concealed qualities with unique gifts and powers that are hidden behind the obvious ones.

Step back and take a good view of your achievements. Don't look at the things you feel you've failed with. There are never failures but mere chances for betterment. This is where you'll have to really hold firm to the proposed goals and reasons for them.

Don't be disheartened and don't be afraid! Continue doing what you're doing. It's in those moments when you feel like surrendering and are about to quit when your breakthrough comes. So, grasp for it and hold on.

Give yourself a special treat, as you've worked hard and merit it. Remember, even if there's no one around who sees the vision you have, put favorable things in your sight at all times to remind you of the achievements you've made up to now.?

You are able to hear this inspirational song here:

http://www.youtube.com/watch?v=nsUdZrG1Fpo

Wrapping Up

Lastly, the mending might of inspirational music, to me, likewise comes from its power to open our hearts. There are songs and tunes that open our hearts to feelings that we didn't even recognize we were closed to! We may listen to something that brings us to tears when we weren't feeling sad. This may be through a connection to Universal sorrow or to our own personal grief.

The same is true of delight. A song may make us recognize, "that's what I needed!" While we had no idea. We don't recognize what we suppress inside, till it's been set free and we feel the sense of alleviation, purifying, and refilling.

Music joins us to the indefinable, the sublime, and the matchless that we long to reconnect with. With or without words.

So search your music world. Shut your eyes and truly hear it. And then open yourself up and let the music urge you on.

www.ingramcontent.com/pod-product-compliance
Lightning Source LLC
LaVergne TN
LVHW021328200726
843509LV00014B/2432